THE STATION SIGNAL BOXES AND OTHER BUILDINGS

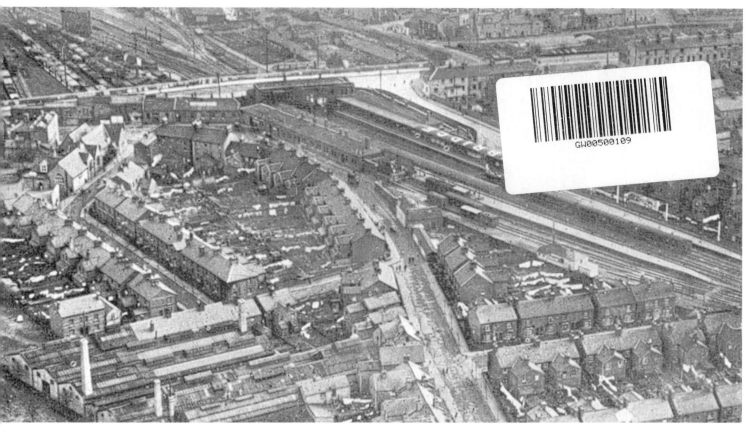

A superb ariel view of the station at Tonbridge around 1910-20. Clearly shown are the three sidings on Barden Road side and the signal box by the east yard, or down sidings.

TONBRIDGE: THE STATION

Opened on 26th May 1842 by the South Eastern Railway. Principal engineer of the line was William Cubit who was probably responsible for the design of the station buildings as well.

The Medway was utilised for transport of all ballast, sleepers and rails and a temporary wharf was constructed within 50 yards of the rail head.

Betts was the contractor employed to oversee construction of the line and by November 1841 the first track was laid. During the winter all track was finally in position and the line subsequently opened.

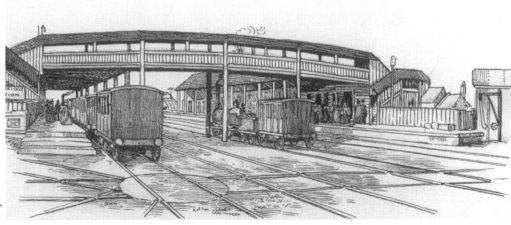

The station on its original site before rebuilding, is seen from an early print. (A. Giles)

Front cover:
'The Buddicorn Locomotive' shown here at Tonbridge prior to making its way to the Festival of Britain (South Bank) in 1951. Designed and built by the English engineer William Buddicorn at 'Les Chartreux', near Rouen, Normandy, in 1844, numbered 3 and given the name 'Saint Pierre'. Converted into a tank engine before being rebuilt by the Sottenville Cuatre-Mares works in 1946 to its original form, along with a new tender. Although carrying No. 3 it is not original as this number but in the main No. 33 with parts from other locomotives of the class incorporated.

(K. Glascott) Information supplied by the NRM York.

Back cover:
H class No. 31533 with the 4.04pm Tonbridge to Oxted and return descends the bank with a push pull train on 24th March 1962. Push pull operating is where the driver can operate the train from either the locomotive or the leading coach. This leaves the fireman to look after the engine, as in this case where the driver is in control at the front end.

(L.W. Rowe)

THE STATION AND THROUGH TRACK

This shows single canopy on both platforms and a bay where platform 1 now is. 1888.

(Lens of Sutton

Telegraph poles are now in evidence along with the through line on platform 1 and much wider platforms. 1940-50.

(Lens of Sutton

ird rail now in along with different lighting and me boards. Telegraph poles removed. 1983.

PLATFORMS 3 AND 4

As can be seen from these two photos very little has changed over the years. This one shows the station about 1910. (Lens of Sutton)

he station in 1983. (Lens of Sutton)

ENGINE SHED (MPD), TURNTABLE, COAL STAGE, GOODS SHED AND WATER TOWER

At the same time as the building of the station the engine shed was constructed, but as a three road single ended one. It was not until much later that t
SER carried out alterations, the new depot consisting of a six road brick building with a slated roof. In 1952 the shed roof was completely reconstructe
the pitched roof being replaced with a flat asbestos one and the gable ends greatly reduced. The photo shows the MPD in 1963. Loco in the foreground w
cover on chimney is an 'N' class. On 4th January 1965 the shed was closed, demolition taking place in 1968/9 leaving the walls and offices that we
removed in 1984.   (L. Twyma

The original turntable was located somewhere in the front of the shed to the right (Tunbridge Wells side) of the coal stage. It was then moved to the sou
side of the shed in the junction formed by Priory Road and Strawberry Vale Bridge. Diameter of this turntable was 54ft 9in.   (L. Twyma

The coaling stage with its loading crane. Sometime in 1963.   (L. Twyman)

e goods shed was built around the turn of the century replacing a row of ̶tages. Over the years it was a hive of activity with horse and cart used to ̶t with, these being replaced by 3-wheeled 'mechanical' horses, as they ̶e known, moving masses of items daily. This photo shows it as it was in ̶3 used as a backdrop to the ever encroaching car park. Sadly it has now ̶e, replaced by more car parking spaces.

̶ water tower was built around the turn of the century and to start with was ̶k based. Situated alongside Vale Road it must have appeared to be at least ̶ high from the road but from the trackbed was probably not more than ̶ high. Around 1930 the original one was demolished and the one here ̶n was built. This was fed with water from Sevenoaks tunnel via a network ̶ipes and as this was spring water would have been a lot softer than mains ̶efore causing less scale deposits in the boilers. Its vicinity to the local ̶tball and cricket ground must have made this an ideal vantage point for ̶ching Tonbridge at home and Kent Cricket Club's matches.   (A. Clifton)

SIGNAL BOXES

West 'A' Box was one of two built on this site. The first being an all timber construction, where as this one is of brick and timber. Trains passed through the base of the original box and signals were fixed to the top for ease of operation. (A.E. Bennett)

The interior of 'A' box showing the large amount of levers (80) and also the track layout on the wall. (P. Bartholomew)

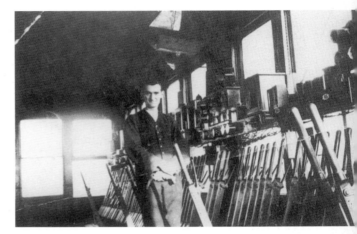

The interior of 'B' box showing the mass of levers needed to control all the signals and points in the surrounding area. This box had 90 levers. Signalman is George Stedman. (P. Bartholomew)

East 'B' box straddled the siding near to the coal yard. The original signal box stood over the down main line on the opposite side near to the goods shed. (J. Head)

This view shows the 'B' box being demolished some time in the mid sixties. (B. Clifton)

RAILWAY ACCIDENTS

he first accident occurred in 1846 at the Weir Bridge, a wooden structure which, due to heavy rain and flooding was washed away. This led to a train rom London plunging into the gap. The fireman is reported to have died ree days later. This accident is recorded as being the first known one in the istory of the railway in Britain.

'The next accident, on 28th May 1878, involved No. 99 while acting as station pilot at Tonbridge. The driver had signed on at 9.30am and worked a cattle train to Redhill, returned with empty wagons to Tonbridge, then taken the 2.40pm coal train to Tunbridge Wells and collected wagons from the LB&SCR station before returning to Tonbridge. There, No. 99 was to

act as up side pilot until the crew signed off at 10.45pm, after being on duty for 13¼ hours. As this time approached the driver, without authority from the signalman, positioned his engine at the east end of the up platform near the road bridge where it was run into at 20mph by the 18-carriage 7.30pm Dover–Charing Cross express travelling at 20mph headed by '118' class 2-4-0 No. 26. Again the collision was violent, but no deaths occurred for much of the impact was absorbed by No. 99's tender and three mail vans at the front of the express.'

From 'The Locomotive History of the South Eastern', an RCTS publication by D.L. Bradley.

909 ACCIDENT

om a postcard issued by W. Gothard of Barnsley who specialised in ilway 'disaster' type cards.

Collision involving two SECR 4-4-0 'E' class locomotives

'Accidents involving the class were fortunately few and far between while those that did occur were comparatively minor. The one of note was at Tonbridge on the morning of 5th March 1909 and involved Nos. 165 and 497. The latter was in charge of the 8.40am Cannon Street–Dover Town via Redhill and was approaching the junction of the Sevenoaks and Redhill lines at Tonbridge when the driver observed the down home signal to be partially lowered. Under the circumstances he should have stopped and requested advice from the nearby signalbox, but instead he increased speed and passed the signal. Then to his horror he noted that an up main line express was signalled and realising his error he put on more steam to get across before a collision occurred. Unfortunately, he gave no thought to the down main line along which No. 165 was approaching the junction with the 9.05am Cannon Street–Dover Pier mail express under clear signals and at 25 to 30mph. The crew had no reason to anticipate trouble, but standing on the right side of No. 165's footplate Driver Stevenson

suddenly became aware of a train converging on him. At once he applied the brakes, but to no avail for at 20mph No. 165's leading end crashed into the intruder, derailing No. 497 and three vans as well as scattering wreckage across all four lines. No. 165 and four GPO vans were also derailed while some 150 yards of track was severely damaged and all the west box signalling made inoperative. In a few brief moments before this occurred the signalman, appreciating that an accident was unavoidable despatched a warning to the east box which gave that signalman time to pull his signals to danger and stop No. 36 and the 7.45am Margate Sands–Cannon Street express. This train was not booked to stop at Tonbridge and being 12 minutes late was approaching the junction with the Hastings branch at about 40mph when the driver saw the home signal go to danger. He immediately shut off steam and braked heavily, but was not able to stop until clear of the roadbridge at the east end of the station and some 100 yards from the wreckage. Casualties were remarkably light and would have been much less if No. 497's fireman and an inspector travelling on the footplate had not attempted to jump clear and been run over and killed.'

From 'The Locomotive History of the South Eastern and Chatham Railway', an RCTS publication by D.L.Bradley

From a series of photographs by H.H. Camburn of Tunbridge Wells. This shows SECR 'E' class coppertop No. 165 involved in the railway disaster on 5th March 1909 in which two workers were killed and eleven injured. Note the engine still carries its original SER No. (R. Smith)

Many officials appear in this photo, including the station master in his top hat (centre of photo). (Lens of Sutton)

Part of the crowd who turned up to watch the work involved in clearing up after the crash. Services resumed early next morning. (Lens of Sutton)

A pair of unknown stirling F1 class locomotives with 7ft driving wheels haul a rake of nine six-wheeled carriages up the long bank towards Somerhill tunnel about 1900. Both still appear to carry original cabside plates but only the rear locomotive has SE&CR on its tender side. (Author's collection)

Shown here is one of James Stirling's F class 4-4-0s with 7ft driving wheels. No. 118 was built at Ashford in 1895 and was allocated to Dover. In 1899 it was allocated to Tonbridge where it is seen still bearing its SER cabside number plate but sporting SECR on its tender sides. Rebuilt at Ashford in 1908 it remained a Tonbridge engine until 1924 when it was transferred to Reading until withdrawal in May 1933. (C. Martin)

The same locomotive is seen here after rebuilding. Gone is the old SER number plate to be replaced by a SECR one and with its number painted on the tender. The boiler is now domed and has a shorter chimney. Other changes were a longer firebox (2in), more tubes (5), a larger grate area and more working pressure (20lb). (C. Martin)

Southern Railway Schools Class 4-4-0 No. 905 'Tonbridge' stands on shed soon after outshopping from Eastleigh in May 1930. The 'E' prefix was dropped between May and June 1931. Known staff are Bert Stapley standing by left buffer and George Goldsmith second from right, standing.

Seen here about 1915 is P class 0-6-0 No. 323, one of eight built. No. 323 entered traffic from Ashford works in July 1910 and was allocated to Orpington. Withdrawn in June 1960 it was sold to the Bluebell Railway in 1960/1 along with No. 178.

N class 2-6-0 No. 810 was the first of its class to be built at Ashford, entering service on 19th August 1917. It was soon to be seen at Tonbridge where it stayed for lengthy periods so that a team from Ashford could make weekly inspections and report any design or equipment changes before the class was augmented. Withdrawal took place in March 1964. It is seen here on shed in the mid twenties, with some of the loco staff. Those known are J.B. Holman, R. Ashdown and Cliff Martin (left, standing).

(C. Martin)

Neatly framed by the signal gantry and with 'SOUTHERN' still on its tender is Schools class No. 900 'Eton' (BR No. 30900) August 1948. One wonders what the driver of 'Eton' and the railway worker were discussing.

(G.E. Mortley)

Racing through the station with the 'Golden Arrow' and as yet still not named is West Country class No. 21C137 (BR No. 34037) August 1948. this locomotive was eventually given the name 'Clovelly' and was rebuilt by BR in 1958.

(G.E. Mortley)

D class 4-4-0 No. 31734 as built by Sharp Stewart and Co. in April 1901. It was reboilered at Ashford works in 1914 where it stayed working from until allocated to Tonbridge in 1931. No. 31734 is seen here sporting lined black livery as applied in July 1950. Withdrawal took place in October 1955 after a total mileage in service of over 1,000,000 miles.

(D. Bassett)

Standard 2-6-4T No. 80018 arrives at Tonbridge with the 1.05pm train from Redhill on 19th August 1953. H class No. 31193 stands in the bay with a train of vans.

(J. Head)

13

LNER BI No. 61274 with the 9.39am Bickley to Margate leaving Tonbridge on 7th June 1953. This was one of the locos loaned to Southern Region while the Bulleid Pacifics had been temporarily withdrawn. (B.I. Fletcher)

C class No. 31585 makes hard work of the climb out of Somerhill tunnel, as it heads towards Tunbridge Wells West yard with a train load of coal on 9th June 1954. (B.I. Fletcher)

Tonbridge MPD (74D) with a good number of locomotives present, those easily recognised are D1 No. 31489; L No. 51763; Q1 No. 33033 and H No. 31259 along with another Q1 and two C class (D. Ingram)

Standing short of the coaling stage at Tonbridge MPD is N class 2-6-0 No. 31866, Monday 26th September 1955.   (B. J. Miller)

H class tank No. 31326 shunting goods at Tonbridge in 1955.   (B.J. Miller)

D1 class 4-4-0 No. 31145 stands in light steam to the rear of the shed on 26th September 1955.

(B.J. Miller)

Billington E3 class 0-6-2T No. 32456 on shed along with an unidentified C class. Behind, in light steam, is Q1 class No. 33029, 1955. (B.J. Miller)

H class No. 31548 on shed, 26th September 1955.

(B.J. Miller)

Mid 1957 view at the front of the shed with N class No. 31879 preparing for duty. Another N class No. 31406 simmers gently while to the rear a C class No. 31686 makes its way to the turntable.

(D. Ingram)

King Arthur class 4-6-0 No. 30769 'Sir Balan', one of the class built by the North British Locomotive Company in 1925, heads an up boat train through Tonbridge on 28th July 1956.

(A.E. Bennett)

British Rail class 5 No. 73081 passing through Tonbridge with a down express on 28th July 1956. One of the class No. 73082 'Camelot' is preserved at the Bluebell Railway.   (A.E. Bennett)

A clean H class No. 31543 (74D Tonbridge) stands at the front of the shed on 9th March 1957.
(F. Hornby)

C class No. 31585 (74D Tonbridge) on shed, to the rear an unidentified N class takes on coal, 9th March 1957.   (F. Hornby)

Of all the 4-4-0s ever built the Schools were thought to be one of the more powerful. Here we see No. 30936 'Cranleigh' on the turntable at Tonbridge MPD on 9th March 1957.   (F. Hornby)

H class No. 31193 (74D Tonbridge) stands with funnel covered, out of use at the rear of the shed, along with L class No. 31773 on 9th March 1957.
(F. Hornby)

Sporting Tonbridge's 74D shed plate former LBSC 'E3' No. 32456 stands in the rear shed sidings along with sister engine No. 32454 on 9th March 1957.   (F. Hornby)

One of the many of Maunsells rebuilding of locomotives of the Wainwright design is the D1. Built in 1901 to work boat train and other main line expresses they were much liked by drivers as they were good 'steamers'. This locomotive No. 31739 was rebuilt in 1927 at Ashford and is seen here on the turntable at Tonbridge on 11th May 1957.
(F. Hornby)

L class No. 31773 takes on coal while H class No. 31184 waits for its turn, 11th May 1957. The L was one of the class built by A. Borsig of Germany, which was shipped over in parts and assembled at Ashford under the supervision of Borsig fitters.
(F. Hornby)

Merchant Navy 4-6-2 No. 35028 'Clan Line' passing through with the 10.00am Victoria to Dover boat train on 11th May 1957.
(F. Hornby)

Engineering works at Tonbridge on 27th April 1958. This was remodelling of the track for future electrification and ease of operation. The train coming up on the wrong line is the 12.33pm Redhill to Tonbridge hauled by N class No. 31407. (B.I. Fletcher)

King Arthur class No. 30806 'Sir Galleron' approaching with a local stopping train on 15th September 1957. (A.E. Bennett)

H class 0-4-4T No. 31193 shunts empty stock into the west yard in May 1958.   (F. Rowley)

Battle of Britain No. 34085 '501 Squadron' heads a down coastal express through Tonbridge in May 1958.   (F. Rowley)

View from the roadbridge as King Arthur class No. 30801 'Sir Meliot de Logres' approaches with a train from the Kent coast on 3rd May 1958.
          (A.E. Bennett)

Britannia class 4-6-0 No. 70004 'William Shakespeare' heads an up 'Golden Arrow' through Tonbridge on 3rd May 1958.　　(A.E. Bennett)

Climbing the bank out of Tonbridge with an Oxted train is C class 0-6-0 No. 31716, January 1960.
(B.J. Miller)

The driver of H class No. 31512 poses for the camera as he shunts empty stock through the station, 1960.　　(B.J. Miller)

Nearing Tonbridge with the 'Golden Arrow' is Battle of Britain No. 34086 '219 Squadron' on 2nd January 1960.　　　　(D.K. Jones)

With its back to the camera Schools class 4-4-0 No. 30928 'Stowe' stands on shed on 8th May 1960.
　　　　(B.J. Miller)

H class No. 31500 at the coaling plant on 2nd September 1960. To the left behind the coal plant can be seen the water tower which was much a part of the landscape around south Tonbridge. From Vale Road it appeared to be at least 50ft high, although it was probably more likely only between 25 and 30ft high from the trackbed.

(R. Picton)

Battle of Britain class No. 34088 '213 Squadron' heads the 'Golden Arrow' through Tonbridge on 2nd September 1960.   (R. Picton)

H class No. 31533 stands back to back with H class No. 31543 at the rear of the shed on 2nd September 1960.   (R. Picton)

Tonbridge's vast allocation of steam locomotives seems somewhat diminished here (65 at this date) with only H class No. 31518: Q1 No. 33029: N1 No. 31880 and C class No. 31719 visible, along with an unidentified H class in the background, 2nd September 1960.   (R. Picton)

Although built in 1904 the H class survived well into the sixties. They were neat and attractive robust tank locomotives well suited to secondary passenger duties, and in later years many of the class were fitted for push and pull operation. Here No. 31542 is seen on shed on 2nd September 1960.
(R. Picton)

C class No. 31719 on shed 2nd September 1960. Tonbridge crews were well known for keeping their locomotives clean, as can be seen from the appearance of this one.   (R. Picton)

Another of the popular H class tanks of which 66 were built. This one No. 31512 survived until 1961 and is seen here on shed on 5th September 1960.
(R. Picton)

Q1 class No. 33035 on the turntable which was situated to the south side of the shed. These powerful and useful locomotives were used mainly for heavy freight although in later years they did haul passenger trains. (R. Picton)

U1 class No. 31902 stands in the station with a local stopping train on 5th September 1960.
(R. Picton)

Bullied Q1 class No. 33035 heads an up freight through Tonbridge station on 5th September 1960.
(R. Picton)

Late afternoon sunshine throws shadows onto the platform as H class No. 31553 waits with a two coach train for the Dunton Green/Westerham service, 5th September 1960.   (R. Picton)

At the head of the 3.46pm to Ashford is Schools class No. 30915 'Brighton', 5th September 1950.
(R. Picton)

Rebuilt West Country class No. 34101 'Hartland' heads an up express through Tonbridge, while O1 class No. 31065 and C class No. 31592 wait to leave with an LCGB railtour on 11th June 1961.
(A.E. Bennett)

Tonbridge MPD (73J) on 16th June 1961 with O1 class No. 31065 at the coal stage and L1 class No. 31786 along with N1 class No. 31877 at the front of the shed. The L1 appears to have been given a coat of paint on its front buffer beam and buffers, along with a good clean, prior to working a special.
(A.E. Bennett)

L class No. 31749 along with H class No. 31308 back down towards the station to pick up stock for a special on 11th June 1961. (A.E. Bennett)

Q1 class 0-6-0 No. 33030 stands by the oil tank at Tonbridge MPD on 21st August 1961. This class of locomotive had many nicknames including: Charlies, Coffee Pots and just plain 'Ugly'.
(D.K. Jones)

2-6-4T No. 80038 climbs the bank towards Somerhill tunnel with the 4.10pm train to Eastbourne via Tunbridge Wells West on 16th September 1961.
(D. Trevor Rowe)

2-6-4T No. 80151 approaching with a train from Eastbourne via Tunbridge Wells on 16th September 1961. This locomotive is preserved.
(D. Trevor Rowe)

N1 class 2-6-0 No. 31878 on shed 16th September 1961, to the right stand C class No. 31592 and H class No. 31177.

(R. Picton)

Schools class No. 30929 'Malvern' on shed, 16th September 1961. This was one of the class fitted with multiple jet blastpipe and larger diameter chimney. (R. Picton)

2-6-4T No. 80066 climbs the bank out of Tonbridge with the 5.10pm Brighton train on 16th September 1961. (L.W. Rowe)

N1 class No. 31822 approaching with a train from Brighton via Eridge on 16th September 1961. This engine was the only three cylinder version of the class, although numbered within the N class series this was the prototype for the N1 class, which it was reclassified to. (D. Trevor Rowe)

31

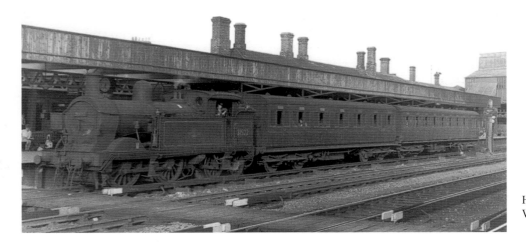

H class No. 31522 with a Maidstone West–Tonbridge train on 16th September 1961.
(D. Trevor Rowe)

Stored out of use at the rear of the shed H class No. 31177 has only a short life left. Seen here on 16th September 1961 it was to survive until October. One of the class, however, has survived (No. 31263) and can be seen at the Bluebell Railway.
(R. Picton)

H class 0-4-4T No. 31161 nearing Tonbridge with a train from Tunbridge Wells West on 16th September 1961. (D. Trevor Rowe)

N1 class No. 31822 heads the 6.10pm Tonbridge to Brighton train up the bank towards Somerhill tunnel on 16th September 1961.   (L.W. Rowe)

Built originally in 1925 as a 2-6-4 tank 'River Test' this locomotive was rebuilt as a 2-6-0 in 1928 due to the rolling at speed. Mileage covered as a tank engine was nearly 70,000. Seen here as converted to a 2-6-0 in 1962 it survived until February 1965 and was broken up by Buttigegs of Newport.
(B. Clifton)

N1 class 2-6-0 No. 31876 stands out of use with chimney covered on 24th March 1962. Only six of this class were built. No. 31876 survived until November 1962 and was broken up at Eastleigh works.   (B.J. Miller)

Charlie Pettit, foreman fitter, and George Warner putting a new bogie on H class No. 1193 at Tonbridge loco 1935.   (G. Warner)

Q class 0-6-0 No. 30549 on shed undergoing light repairs to its cylinders. Note the piston rings and nuts on strings on the buffers, 1952. (L. Twyman)

An unidentified N class locomotive waits on shed for attention by a boilersmith sometime in the mid fifties.

(Vic Young)

Boilermakers Les Twyman and 'Tich' Howarth prepare to fit a new flue tube to the boiler of an unidentified Q1 class locomotive. Note that to make the job easier the smokebox door has been taken off completely. Date around 1956-1963. (L. Twyman)

With connecting rod removed and bearings on the frame in front of the splasher H class No. 31530 stands out of use awaiting repairs on 21st August 1961. This locomotive had only a short life left as it was cut up at Ashford works in March 1962. (D.K. Jones)

RAILWAY EMPLOYEES OF THE FORMER SOUTH EASTERN RAILWAY, SOUTH EASTERN AND CHATHAM RAILWAY, SOUTHERN RAILWAY AND BRITISH RAILWAY

Drivers, Firemen, Guards, Ticket Collectors, Office Staff, and other employees of the old South Eastern and Chatham Railway. Date about 1910.
Names known are F. Bluden (Guard), Mr Gutteridge (Office), D. Simmonds (Driver), Richardson (Guard), F. Holland, Mr Sheldrake (Running Foreman).
(Mrs Holman)

Hayman Herbert Frank
Entered Service 14 June 1917   at 14/- Per Week
Appointed 13 January 1919   Date of Birth 4th Dec 1900
                                    Passed Doctor 18/6/17

Maidstone West	Carriage Cleaner		14 - 6 - 17	14/- Per Week Temp
"	"	Engine Cleaner	11 - 3 - 18	1/8 Per Day
"	"	" "	7 - 12 - 18	2/- " "
"	"	" "	13 - 1 - 19	2/- " " Appoint
"	"	" "	18 - 8 - 19	6/- " "
		Firing		9/6 " "
				Joined D.F.R? 17-1?
Transferred to Battersea			22 - 1 - 23	9/6 Per Day
Appointed Fireman			5 - 3 - 23	" " "
— "	Fireman		- 6 - 23	10/6 " "
Transferred to Maidstone	"		3 - 25	11/- " "
Transferred to Tonbridge	"		17 - 7 - 33	12/- Per Day
Passed Driving Test			29 - 4 - 41	12/- " "
" Doctor	Passed Fireman		12 - 5 - 41	12/- " "
	Driving		" " "	13/- " "
Appointed Driver at Tonbridge			11 - 9 - 44	13/- " "

This shows the service record of Frank Hayman and the rates of pay on each transfer and appointment.
(J.E. Turner)

TONBRIDGE MOTIVE POWER REPAIR SHOP STAFF

Shed Masters
J. Downer, E. Wardman.
Running Shed Foremen
Sid Laurence, Sid Lucas, H. Corke, F. Dawes, T. Luckett, J. Randle.
Fitting Staff
J. Blackwell, J. Stevens, M. Wright, C. Lefevre, R. Coleman, B. Thompson, C. Wright, W. Ritchie, A. Robinson, K. Mockeridge, T. Willard, H. England, B. Maynard, C. May, F. Saunders, G. Gorridge, T. Hewitt, H. Southern, G. Holmes, B. Baker.
Boilermakers
L. Twyman, L. Yeomanson, G. Primmer, J. Eskdale, J. Colville, 'Tich' Howarth.
Boilerwashers
H. Green, B. Palmer.
Foreman Fitter
Charlie Pettit.
Firelighter
Ernie Miller.
Steam Crane Drivers at Coal Stage
Wally Bellingham, K. Drury.
Cleaning Foreman/Chargeman
Chas Mercer.
Shedmen
B. Bradford, G. Judd, K. Jury, H. Cooper, P. Brown.
Storesman
P. Pankhurst, B. Girling, L. Tasker.
Time Clerks
W. George, B. Roberts, Wally Bellingham (finished service at this post).
Office Staff
J. Mathers, C. Bissenden, J. Bridger.
Shop Office Man
J. Reeks (ex driver) and garden expert.

A member of BR's railway policemen, Mr Harold Etchells, poses for the camera somewhere in the east yard, or down sidings area about 1950.
(Hazel Glascott)

A group of railway employees pose for the camera in 1951. They are, left to right: Brian Allchin, Driver Frank Thorn and Fireman Ken Glascott.
(K. Glascott)

Some of the uniform and clerical staff of the former SECR pose for the camera at Tonbridge Goods Depot soon after the First World War (about 1920). Those known are, back row, left to right: Atterton, Jim Vant, A. Ridge, unknown, E. Smith, unknown, C. Martin, Bob Starnes. Front row, left to right: Sid Burrows, unknown, Fred Pegden, unknown. Mr Ridge's father is third from left, back row. (J. Ridge)

Schools class 4-4-0 No. 905 'Tonbridge' in the upper coal yard sidings during National Savings Week, June 1943. Among those in front of, and on the locomotive are: H. Hayman, D. Catt, Johnstone (loco foreman), B. Catt, T. Lucket, F. Large and S. Smith. (J. Turner)

Ken Lidlow
Ken started on the Southern Railway at Tonbridge in May 1940 as a signal lad in the west 'A' box. After a spell in the Royal Navy he returned to duty as a porter, shunter, guard and finally retired in 1989 as Station Supervisor.   (Ken Lidlow)

Group of fireman/drivers pose for the camera in front of a W class 2-6-4T Tonbridge loco about 1936. They are, back row: A. Hollands, Stokes, R. Laws, J. Cheeseman. Front row: G. Warner, J. Green.   (G. Warner)

Arthur Wells
Arthur joined the Southern Railway on 24th January 1949 as a cleaner at Tonbridge loco. He passed as fireman in September 1959, was appointed driver in 1965 and retired from the railway in March 1990 after 41 years' service. The driver to Arthur's left is Horace Clifton.

(Arthur Wells)

41

Bill Back
Driver Bill Back is seen here on the footplate of H class 0-4-0T No. 31551 sometime in the fifties.

Ian Russell
Ian joined the SR in 1944 and was appointed as a driver in 1954 leaving the railway in 1962 to emigrate to Australia.

(D. Ingram)

Norman Collins
Tonbridge driver Norman Collins at his job of firing before he took up his position as full driver.

(D. Ingram)

Vic Young
Vic started on the Southern Railway in 1948 as a cleaner at the MPD, becoming a fireman (passed) in 1954. His appointment to the position of driver was on 30th May 1966 and after 41 years' service he retired in April 1990.

(D. Ingram)

Stan Blackman
Stan joined the railway with BR in the early fifties but left probably in the sixties. He was a fireman but it is not known if he ever became a full driver.

(D. Ingram)

Dennis Ingram
Dennis joined the Southern Railway on 13th September 1943 and became a fireman in 1944. Was passed as driver on 25th August 1952 and from there in 1966 became an instructor at Stewarts Lane, retiring in 1986 after 43 years' service.

The fireman on the same footplate is Gordon Castle who left the railway in the mid sixties. The locomotive footplate they are both on is Q1 class 0-6-0 No. 33028. (D. Ingram)

Group of platelayers on bank clearing duties around 1940. Those known are 2nd left: Stanford, 4th from left: Fred Lidlow (ganger) and right hand side: Mr Adams.
(Ken Lidlow)

Standing in front of H Class Tank No. 31518 are K. Day, D. White, R. Kitchenham and A. Willett. Date 1958-1960. (D. Ingram)

A. Lambert, F. Clifton, B.W. Tomkinson, Tapp, F. Chick, M. Damper and B. Jennings at Tonbridge Loco around 1968. (D. Ingram)

Labourer in front of furnace at Tonbridge Loco is E. McNally. On left in background is a long handled shovel which was used to carrry hot coals to light up engines. Date 1958-1960. (D. Ingram)

G. Poile, D. Medhurst, F. Laurence and A. Ounstead in front of standard 2-6-4T No.80041 around 1960. (D. Ingram)

Brian Clifton

Brian joined BR in 1951 as a cleaner and started as a fireman on 18th December the same year. He left to do National Service with the RAF from 8th March 1954 to 7th March 1956 and then returned to the railway to continue his service. Appointed as fireman 23rd May 1955, passed for driving on 7th May 1961 and was appointed as a driver on 1st August 1966.

(B. Clifton)

Alan Clifton, Fred Wolfe and Lou Corke enjoy a good laugh as they unload a roll of roofing felt from a box van onto a Scammell three-wheeled 'mechanical horse' in 1962.

(A. Clifton)

OTHER RAILWAY RELATED ITEMS

ENGINE LEAVES RAILS: DELAYS HUNDREDS ON WAY TO CITY

SIX trains were delayed or terminated at Tonbridge on Wednesday morning when a light engine which was moving from the locomotive sheds to take a freight train to Redhill was derailed.

Hundreds of City workers were affected, and buses were run from Tonbridge to Tunbridge Wells.

The 5.54 a.m. train from London Bridge to Hastings via Ashford had to be run to Ashford via Hastings; the 9.6 Sevenoaks to Brighton train terminated at Tonbridge; the 6.25 Tonbridge to Brighton train was cancelled.

The 7.27 Redhill to Tunbridge Wells West terminated at Tonbridge, and the Ashford to Cannon Street was delayed for 11 minutes. The 7.20 Night Ferry from Dover to Victoria was delayed for eight minutes.

A steam crane was ordered from Ashford but it was not needed as Tonbridge railway employees were able to re-rail the engine with the aid of jacks.

The freight train was hauled by another engine.

A British Railways official told the "Free Press" an inquiry would be held.

ON Wednesday, sitting in his home relaxing, Mr. Jack Scott, of 184 Vale Road, Tonbridge, said he had worked harder during the past three days at home than he ever did when he was employed by British Railways.

Mr. Scott retired on Saturday from his work as a charge hand at Tonbridge Station.

He started work on the railway as a carriage cleaner thirty-five years ago. Before that he served with the Royal West Kents for six years.

Mr. Scott said that after he and his wife had stayed with their daughter at Dorchester for a few days, he would consider returning to the station as a casual worker.

"Today I have been cook, navvy and gardener and worked really hard," he said.

Mr. Scott is seen here shaking hands in farewell with the stationmaster, Mr. H. S. Tanner.

Two articles from the long closed Tonbridge Free Press. Both appeared on the front cover of the October 2nd edition, 1953.

Mr Johnson
Sir
              388

I am making this
application for extra soap
ration. The soap ration
is not enough to keep
clean with the class of
coal that come to
Tonbridge. Will you
please give this your
best attention
                    Yours Obedient
                         Servants
          Coalman
F. Child   W. Bellingham
H. Bridgeland   H. Southen
A Robinson   J H Gardner.
H Edwards   H C Baker.

This letter just shows the kind of problem which arose during wartime. The coal must have been of a particularly dusty type hence the request for more soap rations.

(B. Clifton)

West Yard shunting derailment in the sixties. Smiling at the camera is Bert Stapely. Also present are Mr Burrows Station Master Mr Parker, Shed Master and Shunter Scott.   (D. Ingram)

The same incident with from left T. Hewitt, 2 Ashford men, in Trilby hat J. Blackwell and 2 other railwaymen.   (D. Ingram)

Telephone Ext. No. 2758.

SOUTHERN RAILWAY

(589)

From STORES DEPARTMENT H.Q.,
        Coal & Oil Section,
        WATERLOO.

To   Loco Foreman,

MY   C.2.   YOUR

Loco Foreman,

Tonbridge.

Date   14th August, 1943.

Coal Wagon 30000.

The Commerical Superintendent, under reference E/C.3/60366 has the above wagon on hand at Tonbridge station without labels.

Please have it inspected and let me know whether the coal is suitable for locomotives.

C. FRANCIS
PER

The type of to and fro letter between stores at Waterloo and the locomotive running department, Tonbridge. This one regarding a coal wagon without labels. Note the reply on a scrap of paper from a duty roster.   (B. Clifton)

Locomotive Running Department,
TONBRIDGE.

Ref:

MY 113.
Your
C.2.

AWJ/LM.

August 17th 1943.

Coal Wagon 30000.

Yours of the 14th instant.

I have inspected the above wagon of coal and find tha it is suitable for use in locomotives.

For: A. W. JOHNSTON.

C. Francis Esq.,
Coal & Oil Section,
WATERLOO.

SOUTHERN RAILWAY

Locomotive Running Supt's Office,
(A) Headquarters Representative,
ASHFORD, KENT.

My Reference HA/114.
Yr.

20th March, 1944.

Loco Foreman,
Tonbridge.

Coal Stacking - Tonbridge.

Referring to recent telephone conversations, as no barrows were available in Ashford Stores arrangements were made for the one available at Brighton to be sent you, and I understand this has been received. I have now placed your requisition 13662 with Ashford Stores for 3 Navvy Barrows to be supplied to you when available.

When the timber to your Order No.60044 is to hand from Ashford Works, will you please let me know what is received, and if satisfactory.

The 12 No.8 shovels requested, have already been supplied.

For A. COBB.

An interesting set of letters between the loco foremen at Tonbridge and loco HQ at Ashford. Main item an order appears to be timber for coal stacking, What the outcome of these was is anyone's guess.
(B. Clifton

AWJ/

March 24th   44.

113.
HA/114.

Coal Stacking - Tonbridge.

Yours of the 20th instant.

9 planks only came to hand from Ashford Works yesterday - but these are old wagon boards, 15'x9"x 2", and whilst they are not in first class condition they will serve the purpose for the time being.

Mr. Gilmore,
Loco H.Q.
ASHFORD.

SOUTHERN RAILWAY   113

SOUTHERN RAILWAY   113

Locomotive Running Supt's Office,
(A) Headquarters Representative,
ASHFORD, KENT.

My Reference HA/114
Yr.   113.

31st March, 19 44.

Loco Foreman,
TONBRIDGE.

Sent 5/4/44

Coal Stacking - Tonbridge.

Yours of the 24th instant. I note your remarks and the type of timber received.

To ensure you have suitable planks for further use will you please send me an M5A. requisition for the following -

Timber, 9" x 3" x 18'0" long.   12 lengths.

I will then approach the Stores Superintendent to see if a suitable hardwood can be supplied from another source.

For A. COBB.